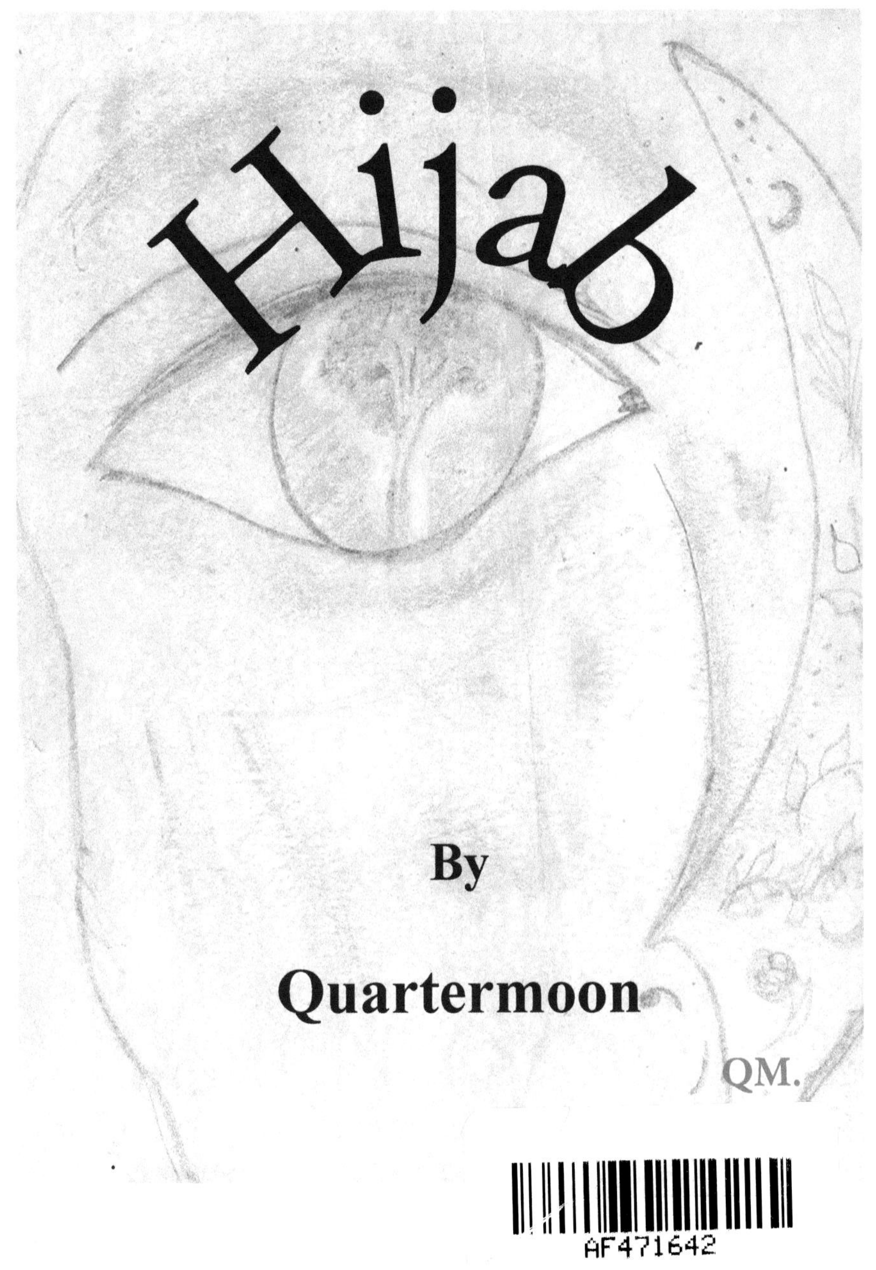
Hijab
By
Quartermoon
QM.

A Passionately Fair Publisher

Manuscript formatting, all interior art work plus cover designing (around the Poets own picture)

By

Pat Simpson

www.apfpublisher.com

ISBN: 978-1-4716-6676-6

Elizabeth Maureen Marquez

Elizabeth AKA "Quartermoon" Poet is a mother of seven and grandmother of seven. Born in the desert of Arizona, on the border of Agua Prieta Mexico, she now resides in Vail, Arizona. Daughter of a full blooded Irish man and a French Cherokee maiden. She attended Eden Valley Medical Missionary Institute, in Loveland Colorado.

Through her much love of poetry and a great need to express her inner most caring thoughts it is therefore no surprise to see this third book come to fruition, her previous two books can be seen with covers portrayed here in the books back pages

Having had her work published in many Anthology's, and Poetry books, both in the US and in the Uk. Quartermoon is now a most well-known respected poet of the present day. See more about this wonderful Poet with her books and video here at her webpage http://apfpublisher.com/QM.html

Contents

Contents

Contents

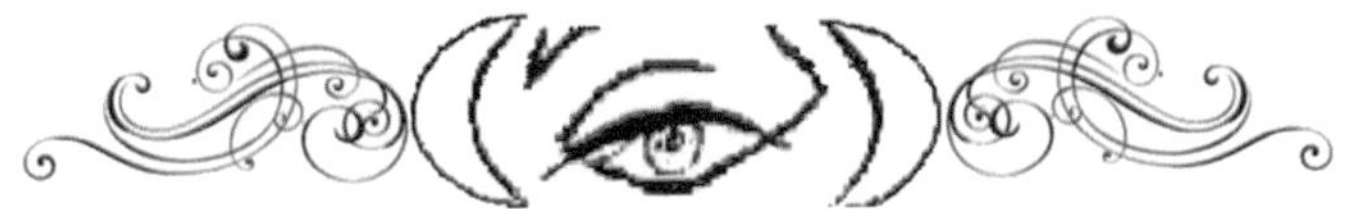

Dedication

This book is dedicated to

Mojgan Imani.

Who has opened my mind

to a greater understanding.

Wishing for Iran

Persia to flow into the future

in God's steed.

Hijab

Seeing her wearing Hijab,
made me think of something Holy

Like a Holy women

An ancient remnant when holiness
meant something

Understanding the Hijab,
and its principles

Teaches me respect and tolerance
of other religions

They wear Hijab outside in public,
so that lust is not

Created in the men

Lust being a sin

But let the women speak of Hijab

Farsinglish

Once there was a Fereshteh.(Angel)

He lived in Behest.(Heaven)

Khoda loved Him.(God)

He sent Him down from Behest to Earth.

"Ou ra dust Darad." He said.(I love you)

Then off to the Earth He went.

He was Setayesh Khoda.(Praising God)

When He died on Earth.

He is a doost , a friend.

A ziad ziba Fereshteh.

Very beautiful Angel.

Tehran / Persia

Wondering what it would be like to be there.
Open wide spaces.
Except for the city,
with tall buildings and congested streets.
Like any city in the USA big and sprawling.

Only it is Tehran.
It's people are beautiful and full of History.
Persia, stories have been told of ancient lifestyles.
Now Persia faces a new world of change,
and understanding.

My Grandmother used to tell me
“Beauty is in the eye of the beholder."
Wishing that everyone can see what I see.
Beauty and eloquent change.

Persian Flower

Persia like inertia
Is moving into the future

It's Farsi they speak
A Persian I did meet

Mojgan is her name
Beauty is her fame

History I'm learning
My heart keeps yearning

For more knowledge to increase
Love will never cease

Medo-Persia and Cyrus the king
Persian music I am starting to sing

Michael the Arc Angel talked to the prince
And Persia has been here ever since

Mojgan said don't worry for war
Someday there will be no more

Because God is taking the lead
His Love please heed

Indeed, indeed!

*This Poem is dedicated Mojgan Imani
Who opened my eyes to a greater understanding!

Political Violence

Political violence is so wrong
Let angels sing this song

Come God and set the matter straight
Give us all Peace and not hate

Oh! The continents and the problems
They go through, 17 year old
Was the first one to die
Jumping over the Berlin wall,
WHO?

Most people don't know
I say woe, woe, woe

Where is the pleasure in life?
Where is the end to strife?

It is a Sacred Secret!

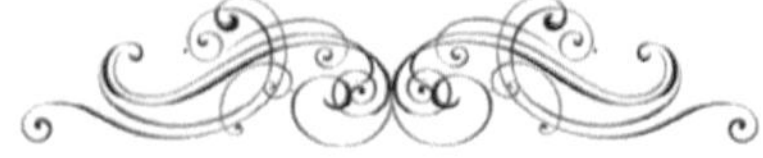

The Snake

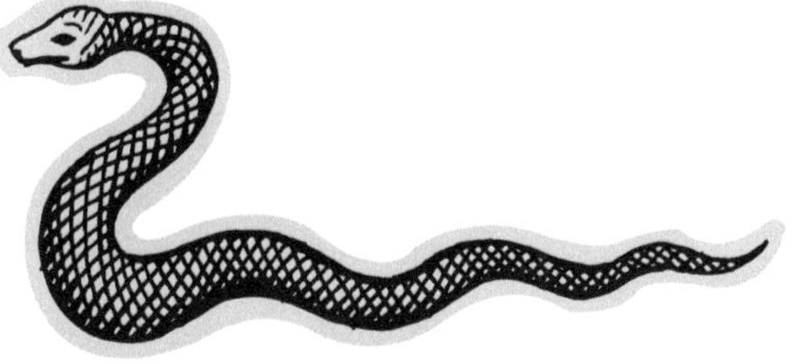

It slithered into our lives.
Deceiving our parents first.

Hark!
What moves in the dark night?

Angel wings take flight.
What Demon that you be?

Ah, to tell you what he has done.
If you meet him run.

His teeth sink in to puncture.
In our lives there is a juncture.

Telling good from evil!

Region of the Dreams

Oh my beloved
How I long for you

You have become the air I breathe
The very smell of the rain is You

Like a cherry tree that blossoms
is my love for You

Let it's fragrance waft in the garden of love
For I have a heart that yearns for You

Kiss me with the kisses of your mouth
Your breath is sweet.

Longing for the day of Your arrival
I am love sick my darling

Refresh me
Take me to the region of the dreams

Speak the Truth

Oh, now you speak your heart?
The truth and only truth,
Speak your heart felt emotions.

Love is the only reason.
Life itself depends on love.
Love is our truth. Gentle, tender,
Forgiving and humble!

Like the sweet fragrant flowers,
So speaks the heart of love!

The Crow

Peck, peck, pecking on the wall outside the bathroom.
A big black Crow was trying to catch someone's attention.

Peck, peck, pecking, each day that went bye.
Curious listeners turn a blind eye.

Impending doom, a disaster coming.
What whispers when the wind blows?

Trouble's coming no one knows.

Tragedy

Tragedy all around us.
How can one be happy if,
the rest of the people are having
a hard time?
Spiritual integrity towards God,
is the answer.
When things are falling down
all around you,
then think on Him.
The one who made the Sun
and the Moon and Stars.
Think on all the beautiful things
He has made.
Even dwell on peace and love.

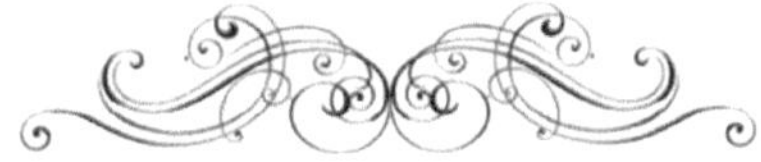

The Beckoning

Down dark corridors of evil,
comes a force, a reckoning.

As God calls our name beckoning.
We rise through the darkness into the light.

There was a war in Heaven, a fight.
Prophecy tells who's won.

Bad Angels they did run.
See the light shine in a dark place.

Our sins we have to face.
Come light take us in.

Clear us of all our sin.

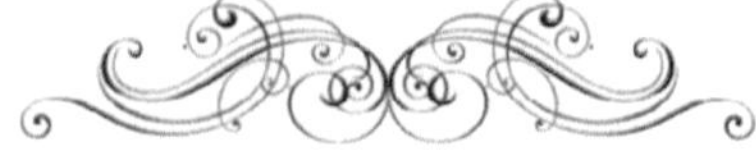

On the Wings of Angels

Ascension, the going up of people,
lifting up into the air.

Ascending

We are all promised ascension by God Himself.
Just think of it.

No more being trapped on planet Earth,.
but allowed to go elsewhere in the Universe.

New friends and family to meet,
wonders of the Universe to discover.

To fly in the arms of the Angels.

Planetesimals

Laying down, and as I fell asleep.

I dreamt that I was in deep, dark, dense space.

When all of a sudden there was a big explosion.

And pieces of fire shot out every which way.

Then started forming planets.

Waking up amazed and awe inspired.

I asked God "What does all this mean?"

Later I learned that those fiery pieces are called planetesimals.

Stumbling across an Astronomy book .

I learned it's how planets were formed.

God is there with each and everyone of us,

wanting to share His Universe.

which is awesomely made.

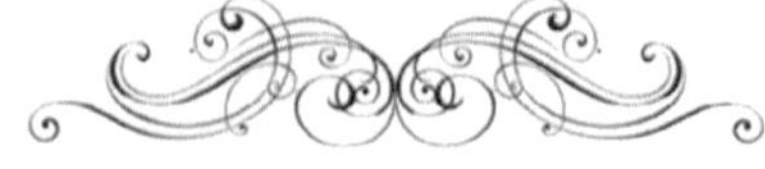

When I Was Alone

I had an epiphany.
Like a pink Carousel.

Shimmering in light.
An ethereal plane.

Laughter and dancing thrill me.
I sink into the light.

And bathe in it's beauty
When I was alone.

Glad We Met

It was a day like any day, when I met Mojgan,
Beautiful Imani

She lives in Persia, the world calls it Iran
Becoming intrigued by her life,

What Persia must be like?
The more I talked to her,

The more Persia became real to me.
God brought my beautiful Mojgan Imani to me.

So we can share our lives.
We are good friends and sisters

Because of Mojgan, I love Persia
We need to realize the beauty that exists in Iran

Look at her History!
My precious Mojgan Imani!

Beautiful people live there.

Hole in the Door

Asleep but my heart was awake.

Feeling like someone holding my hand!

Arousing, finding you holding my hand.

Frightened at first, because of child- hood fears

Of someone under the bed at night!

Holding YOU tightly, I would not let go.

Slipping from my hand I heard your voice say,

"Someone's coming."

You were gone quickly through the dark chasm

That separated us.

GOD How I Love You!

Moon Rays

Looking to love you.
Wanting your love.
King of all life.
Breathe into me peace.
How I love you.
Must tell you so.
Don't ever let me go.
You are my darling.
When the moon looks sad.
I feel your distance.
Not mine but times.
Times, times and half times.
Looking for them to finish.
Like a Jewish mother.
Crying out for her child.
I cry for You.

Adversity

Among the shadowed realm,
lives a shadow.

Hidden from view, on top of her own
But a wisp of a person.

Struggling to make it.
Then one day a vicious one attacks.

Oh shadow among shadows.
Illusive in your realm.

Will you be kind and understanding?
Especially in the face of adversity?

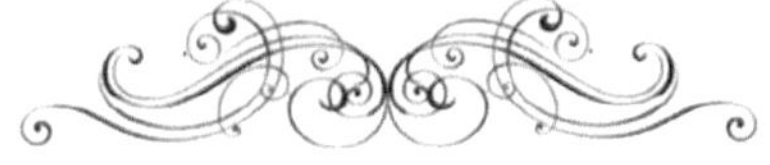

Just To Be With You

A never ending song in my heart.
You are so loving.

Cooing me to your side.
You make me breathless darling.

Do you remember the special moment when we met?
It burns like embers in my heart.

It's you I love , and love only.
When you wrapped your arms around me,

I became awestruck.
Like a bright and shining star you are my beloved.

Little Timmy

Tim is sweet and kind.
As he hides behind his cap ,
sweeping the kitchen floor.

He struggles with Schizophrenia.
Where are you Oh God?
For Tim needs to see you.

A floaty pool ball ,
blows around in the living room.
The fans on.
Someday soon God will answer my
prayers for Tim.

But now he is overcome by his own brain chemistry.

He told me one time .that my face was melting off,
Right as I stood in front of him.
Tim just laughed.

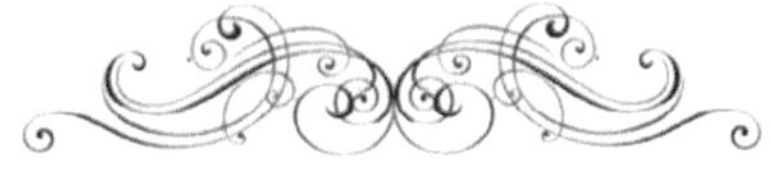

Four Seasons

Spring, Summer, Fall and Winter.
Chopping wood you get a splinter.

Seasons come and then they go.
Inner tubes on blue hued snow.

Rafting by in Summer sun.
Jumping piles of leaves is fun.

In the Spring plants blossom and grow.
Autumn colored leaves, in the wind blow.

Blessings every Season passing.
May your years be filled with laughing!

Awestruck

When I swam in the Sea of Cortez
My mind felt like everything was surreal

The color of the Water was a mystical aqua marine
It was warm

Flying fish flew by
Even seeing a swordfish jump up out of the water

and back in again
Amazing creation's of God's

Awestruck I became

All My Hopes

Wishing for all my hopes.
whispering willows hanging ropes.

Dear one and darling Love penetrates my soul.
God knows you make me whole.

Remembering The Ocean waves.
Memories she saves.

Making sand castles on the beach.
The memories I like to reach.

Touch me darling can't you see.
you are the only one for me.

Whispering Willows blowing in the wind.
Softly blowing leaves across my skin.

Monsoon

The rain is finally here
Peeling thunder, streaks of light

Listening carefully to your voice
Looking for the answers

Waiting for a sign
I will always remember that special day

When You visited me
You and your friends were laughing

A pure happy laugh
It's still raining

I see the light
It reminds me of what You said

"Like lightning coming from out of the East
Shining over the West…"

The Monsoon is here
Thank You

My Friend

I love you more than you know
It is hard to make feelings show

The first time we met
My mind was really set

Then you showed me the way
You had a lot of words to say

Women, you are my friend
Yes, even till the very end

I remember how you talked to me
Your words began to set me free

Oh how I love you
And God does too

Looking for God

When I was a child, I ran away from home.
I was looking for God.

Running away to San Francisco, Berkley,
even Heite, Asbury and Peoples Park.

LOL I looked for him everywhere.
But I could not find him.

Till a day star dawned in my heart.
When I finally found Him. I realized,
That He is inside me.

All I had to do was look inside myself,
to find Him.

He is my Symbiant!

My Mother

Mother, mother
You did hover

Loving me most
Father Son and Holy Ghost

We played tea together
And dolls forever

I remember you mum
Cooking good stuff to give me some

Taking me to church
Watching for those in lurch

You taught me about Jesus
So when He took you from me there were reasons

I always think of calling you
But in Heaven there are no phones.

Night Bird

Sing ever so sweetly
Upon the cloud lit night
Love is in the air,
I won't put up a fight

Always on my mind,
Your trill and sweet song
My lover is coming,
It won't be long

Through lips of one Daughter
Among many, I wait for you
Tenderly slipping through
The Universe for a love so true

When everyone sleeping Night Bird
You sing to me
Telling stories of Love
While you rest in the tree

O'er The Meadow

Down the dirt road,
and into the meadow.
There I ran to meet my Grey headed fellow.

Loves beseeched me,
now I go.
We see each other o'er the meadow.

Echoes of laughter,
and wild flowers so yellow.
In this place soft and mellow.

There I loved my Grey headed fellow.

In The Shade of the Garden

In the shade of the garden rests my love
Oh" by the breath of the morning dawn

As time is relevant, so is my love for You
Because time is yours forever

Slip through my love, in the afternoon rest
Springtime is here again

Let me see Your form
You dwell in light

Now Here It Is

It's just like He said.

Lawlessness will be in abundance,

so far as He said it is true.

The Apostle Paul warned us all,

about this day

and age.

Now here it is!

O A'las

Get in line to make a change.
Journey takes us through a world deranged.

Hold on tight don't let go.
Sanity someday might glow.

When that day comes fast and sure.
All the minds that God will lure.

Priceless day come to pass.
We're with God O'Alas!

Our World in Turmoil

If it were not for our
Jesus, the one called Christ;
I would have no one to follow.

Hardship and despair
All around me.
Surely we live in the last day.

Earthquakes and the like,
One place after another.
Disobedient children,
the world turned sour.

Where is our hope?
It’s in a new world to come.
A promised world.
A new World.

No One

Knocking at the door to my heart.
Opening I got quite a start.

Who is this one so peaceful , calm.
A healing voice a soothing balm.

It's my hearts desire , yes it is.
He gave me what was His.

And in the light I see His face.
No one will ever take His Place.

The Running Man

He found himself running into the desert
Holding a goat sanctified by God

He ran into the desert as far as he could go
It was the goat for Azaziel on Atonement day

He was running so fast the bushes caught his legs
He was doing what his fathers had done before him

Leaving the goat for Azaziel in the desert was the goal
Why does Azaziel get a goat for sacrifice?

Who is Azaziel?

The running man knew it was a demonic creature that needed to be appeased

So he let it go into the desert, and ran back to the encampment
Washing and bathing himself first

I'm warning you little children that these things do exsist
An to do your research on Azazel also named Azaziel

For this is a beginning to enlightenment from Isreal
Atonement Day sacrificing for thousands of years

Why and who is Azazel?

Goodbye Azaziel

Azaziel What have you done?
playing with you is no fun

Fly on prince of the air
You'll be stuck anywhere

I saw you that time when in deep despair
Satan thought to make a lair

My heart is filled with God
Life is like carrying hod

Be strong and get through it
With God we will sit

The Chasm

You did hope upon your mother's breast.

The hope of God.

God took you from your mother's womb.

And from her belly God brought you forth.

He never forsook you.

He never kept you in the grave.

Sheol is a mighty dark pit.

He never left you in it.

Praise God all you people.

Praise His happy and Holy name.

He saved my darling from deaths clutches.

He kept my darling from the dogs

Over The Ocean

Like a storm crossing over the Ocean,
is the world to me.
I look at other nations and I want them to be free.

I already found the answer, for me and for you.
The world is in a depression, what should we all do?

Thinking is the answer, about lives around the world.
They say that Satan on this Earth was hurled.

And if that being the case.
What's in store for the human race?

I believe that God is greater.
I am not a main hater.

Pearls to the swine they say.
And I know the greater way.

The Butterfly

The inner mind.
What does it find?

A journey into many special places.
Death is stasis.

Then a metamorphosis .
like a butterfly.

Beautiful like after morphing
into a glorious form,
Oh my.

Life, Death, and resurrection,
Just like a Butterfly.

The Heart of the Human Race

We look for God.

Knowing who He is

Kind, gentle, and merciful

Our bodies rule us

But it is the Spirit that is supposed to

God says "put away evil"

So shall it be done

God will make sure of it.

To My Jenny

It is my intention to show you, the compassion we must show for the Christ. His death was cruel and brutal. Perpetrated by Godless men. Scoundrels ,oblivious to the truth. He was innocent and they murdered him for no reason. Other than they loved themselves greater than God.

They were bad men waiting for the day of judgment. When everyone answers for their crimes against God himself. The compassion of Christ showed itself in that He became one of us even knowing He would die at our human hands. He is happy to become one of us and is willing to pull us up to His estate in Heaven. This is the reason He comes back, to get us and take us with Him to Paradise New.

Oh, don't think I am crazy.

For the Day of Judgment comes quickly for the ungodly.

But for the children of God it means redemption and freedom at last.

So children keep the love and treasure it as gold
so as no one can take it from you.

Windows

The curtains were put wide open.
It was a look into their lives.

I know why the Lord sent me here.
Because the windows are wide open.

I saw through their pain, and I saw
through their tears.

It was a heavy walk, in life.
Many mountains to cross.

Some times they would walk through the meadows.
But in the last days hardship is rampant,

And the meadows few and far between.
My heart has been touched by their lives.

Like a window I see through them.
They could see me.

If I could say something to help them .
A word at the right moment.

A tender gesture.
Perhaps a shared word from the Lords bosom.

Reminds of the song
*He aint heavy, he's my brother!

Words to Me

When you embraced me and said
"Everything will be alright,"
Happy the woman I am.

Being scared I ran like a rabbit
Into the other room
You are powerful and Mighty

Like a loud trumpet
came your calm voice
It was from on High

Divine my Beloved
Speak with me again
Our darling

Where I'm Dwelling

A shadow
The Dawn

What life I spawn
An ethereal meadow

My mind is reigning in my heart, I live
Now I've become life

A shadow who dwells in my mind in the Gardens
When something dies it withers and hardens

But in my Garden it is freshly blooming all the time.
The choice to dwell there is mine.

Brand New

I heard him say
" I love her soul."

Just the sound of it,
made me whole.

And in the night
when all is calm.

I sit and read
Psalm to Psalm.

Precious words from
a tender mouth spoke.

Love of life,
and filled with hope.

Press close to me darling,
I love you too.

Let us start a Love brand new.

You

You make me love You, by the things You do.
Who You are, is incredible.

No one should have harmed You.
You are my Beloved.

Only You make my heart beat faster.
Thinking of You is the most wonderful
Way spend my mind.

Meditating on You.

You’re Name

Your name is poured out like a perfume.
The wafting draws us to you

That's why the women love You
Come quickly my darling

We are many and we wait for You
Your heart poured out for us

How can we not love
You!

By and By

When the wind blows trough my hair

Feeling as though God is there

When the rain comes pouring down

Knowing God is all around

Thunder, lighting, clouds in the sky

I know you will be here by and by

Floating in Space

Did you ever realize?
That we are floating in space?
On a round rock.

Will we ever capsize?
Moving out of our place.
When we get a knock.

Floating in an endless sea of darkness.
Particles having been thrown out by a big explosion
In space there is no strife.

All the planets there is no starkness.
Super Nova is an implosion
Regenerating life.

The Cook from Planet Mirth

I am a chief Cook in the King and Queen's Castle
Sometimes it turns into a great big hassle

Feed Breakfast , Lunch, and Dinner
Trying to keep the Queen thinner

Snacks and cakes are in between
And the meats gotta be lean

Begrudgingly I feed the Axe Man
The meanest guy in the whole land

Until one day, it was off with my head
The King wishing me dead

For I cooked the pork to rare
Gave the Queen quite a scare

But I'm still here to tell the story
about something that could have been gory

The Jester I'll gladly feed
Because he plants good seed

But the King and Queen aye yaye yaye!
Are going to be fat by and bye!

Conquer

Never had I met a person who had ,
Schizoparanoid, ADHD,
Bipolar and antisocial disorder,
all at the same time.

But then I met you.
Truly diagnosed.
My heart went out to you.

You felt abandoned and unloved.
Then you met me.
Here's hoping you can love me too.

Through Jesus Christ we can do it all,
Together.

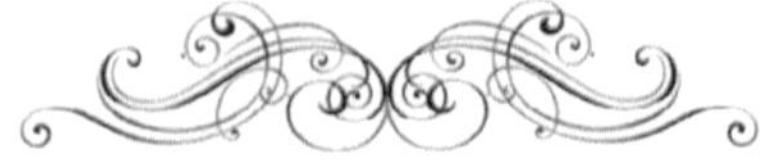

For The Love of Emilia

Oh here you are!

Oh dawn of the morning,

My Emilia!

Your fragrance caused my soul to be spellbound.

Ever in my heart crying out for you.

The day I laid eyes on your tender spirit,

I knew you were mine.

Heart and soul

My Emilia!

God's Whisper

Oh the ocean deep

and then I sink my feet

into the sand

waters spray me as I stand

on the rocks

looking down at my feet

in a shell a little creature I did meet

Amazing this brings a desire never to roam

so tiny carrying it's home.

Eternities Presence

You are my Love and my Dear one.
words are not enough to tell you how I care.
Love stories throughout the ages.

And our love can not be compared.
Our love is like a garden in bloom.
With all it's precious fragrance.

My love is a waterfall.
The ocean breeze.
All these things you are to me.

Embrace me darling .
Never let go.
The answer to Eternities presence

Dark Dungeon

This night in a dungeon I tread.
Bleak Dark room, so no one can see.

Darkness overwhelming.
There is a life for me beyond this dungeon.

Only I can get myself out.
Just God Almighty and I.

He who sees all things.
Even my darkened glooms despair.

Free me God !
Free me now!

Will you take me?
I don't know how.
Dungeon

The Horned Toad

Into my garden you do lurk
Drinking water full of murk

A Dinosaur you look like
Each and every spike

Tiny as can be
Precious sight for me

Graciously we meet
In the garden we seek

I shall always recall
The pleasantries of it all

Grandpa

I never expected for my daughter to take his death so hard.
I never expected for God to pull his card.

We are left here now alone with out him.
The Loneliness creeps in and makes life dim.

When will this pain end, and a fresh outlook come?
It never leaves this pain for even some.

God please bring me rest.
Cuddle me in your nest.

take this pain from me at last.
Let it go and become my past.

Psalm

The world in calm
What a beautiful day

Following a psalm and His Holy Way
Give us spiritual food to learn

Show us how to be calm
Sad for those who burn

Once again following Psalm

Heshbon Eyes

Heshbon Eyes

Like the fish pools in Heshbon
Deep, quiet, clear, and full

Your beauty is beyond compare
East of the River Jordan you lay

My beautiful pools of Heshbon
When you said I had eyes like the
Pools of Heshbon by the gate of Bathrabbim

Knowing it was serene
Calm and full of life

My heart sang
Oh eyes like the pools of Heshbon.

I Am

Four and a half years flew by quickly.
Looking back I lost a lot.

Mentally and Spiritually
No growth was taking place.
Dying inside to be free!

Then one day I am.
What to do with my freedom from oppression.

A degrading of my very being
Was taking place from before.
But now I am.

Pools of Siloam

He was blind, and could not see

But by the pool of Siloam

He was set free

Pool of Siloam bring us memories

Of a time long past

Bring us joy and make it last

Into the water do us cast

I Am Alive

Feeling the wind upon my face.

Knowing one day I'll be in space.

Traveling Interstellar winds.

I've been cleansed of all my sins.

That's why I'm alive.

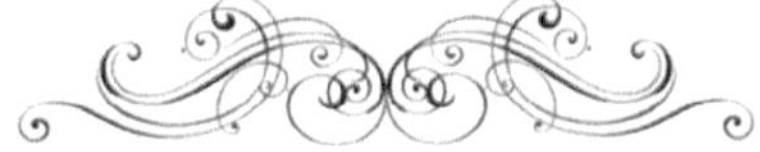

I Could Not Cry

It was not that I did not like him.
Always going out on a limb.

It is what I felt for my life.
I don't want to live in strife.

God's peace is the Holy way.
I want to live it everyday.

When you said Party's over.
I felt like rolling in clover.

You see, I'll go on with my life
Being free from strife.

Tear Drops

I am a tear drop in a storm of rain.
A world of tears for years and years.

Crying at birth's first breath.
We cry because of death.

Keep on looking all your life for what is good.
For sadness and sorrow stay us not.

We are royal warriors in God's Kingdom.
A house of Prince and Princesses.

Storms in life come and go.
So will our tears.

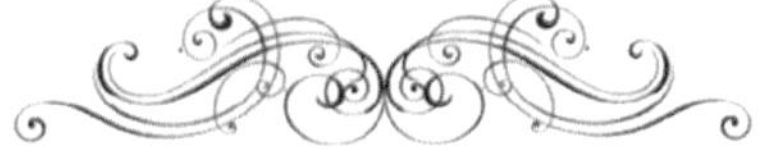

I Am One God

Just as He said He is "one God".
He is not the Sun or the Moon.
He is the creator of such.

Some people say He is more than one God.
But I am here to tell the truth.
He is One.

He makes us one with Him.
He is in us.
All around us speaks of His glory.

He is as you and I are, an individual.
He has feelings just like us.
We are His children.

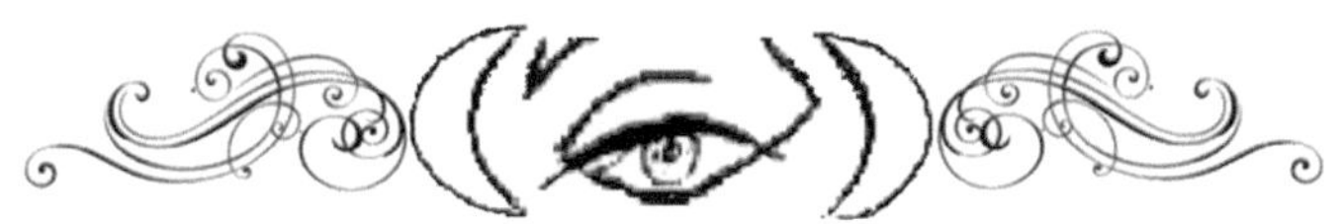

He is one like us.

He is One God.

My sister says He is a woman.

Why deny Him who He is?

He is our Father.

And says "I am one God"

Pray Little Children

Life is what we seek
A good life

Yet so much evil around us
Even children dieing by gun shots

Pray little children pray
Pray for Christ to come

And to come Quickly
"The Spirit and the Bride say come"

" and let him who hears say come"
pray little children pray

Return

Some days my pen fails me.
As the Lord Hails me.

I look into the depths and the height of Gods Kingdom.
Deep far and wide,
Our minds span to places unknown
yet charted questions.

When are you coming back for us?
Take us where you are.

You are deserving of all honor.
We wait for your return.

I Have Been Pondering

I have been pondering life.
There's so much to say.

But no one is listening.
Maybe it is not what I say.

But how I act.
I want to be holy.

My lifes ambition.
What is Holy?

Have we seen a Holy person before
Some guideline.

I use Christ Jesus as my guideline.
All the things said about Him are true.

Even His love.

The personification of a holy man.

How can we not love Him.

Holy is soft and tender.

Let no one break your peace.

The peace you have inside you.

Write On

Writing, because I have something to say.

Something to say about love, life and death.

The beautiful things in between the pages.

Like a rose that is placed in between the pages of a book.

My words live on inside those pages.

Memories, thoughts, dreams.

If there is anything I can leave behind in life.

It would be words of help to those who read on after me.

If I could just leave them a treasure.

Something of value, like real gold.

Spiritual Gold.

So I write on.

Elizabeth's First Book

THE QUARTER MOONPOET

QUARTERMOON

emarquez0623@msn.com

Elizabeth's Second Book

'Sojourners'

By

Quarter Moon

http://apfpublisher.com/QM.html

A.P.F.P. Books By

Poets World-Wide

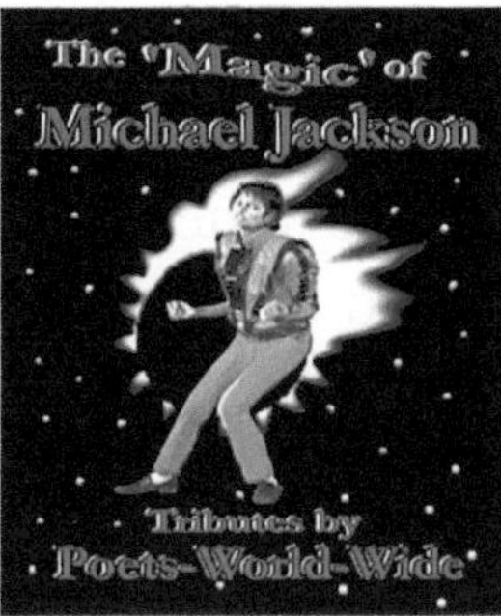

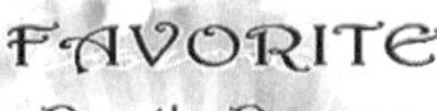

Poet's Poems

2010

Poets World-Wide

Practical Poetic Anthology

A Genuine Glossary of Great Poems

"Styles, Forms & Pageanted Portrayals"

Poets World-Wide

By

Poet's World wide!

A.P. F. P. Authors & Book Titles:

Patricia Ann Farnsworth-Simpson: Windows of Light: Life's Carousel: A Bundle of Muse: The Twinkles: Flick The Karate Pig: Jack the Lad: The Wizard the Witch and Joe the Toe: A Compilation of Tales to Thrill and Chill: Stories To Thrill and Delight: Styles A-Plenty, Embracing Poetry with Style,

Carolyn Sconzo My Garden is Growing:

Christina R Jussaume Amazing Pets & Animals: Spiritual Living Waters: Spiritual Enlightenment: Joseph's Star of Eternal Promise: Spiritual Victory: To God Give The Glory: Spiritual Encouragement

Erich J Goller The Trojan Horse: Groovy: My Candle Kept on Burning: For All Our Tomorrows, Just For The PUN of It Life's Magic Candle

George L. Ellison - Poetic Reminisces:

Jacquelyn Sturge Live, Love Laugh A Lot: Live, Love Laugh With Me Through Poetry A to Z

J. Elwood Davis The Blue Collar Scholar:

Jennifer Lee Wilson Fantasy and Foibles:

Joanne Agee Born To Be A Rebel:

Joe Hartman Pieces of Existence:

John Henson Shadow Dancer I Shadow Dancer II; Broken Wings, The Chronicles of Gildas; Darklingmire:

A.P. F. P. Authors & Book Titles:

Joree Williams Ariella: Living With Cancer:

Kathleen Charnes-Zvetkoff Embroidered Limericks:

Mary Ann Duhart From Out of The Pit I Cried,
Duhart Expressions Writing With Styles,
A Spiritual Breakthrough with Poetry:

Michael L Schuh But It's Mine, The Fruit of My Pen:
Mike and Joe, The Cross, Spiritual Thoughts on Love and Life The Porter Family -Mike's Choice Song Lyrics:
The Shiners Fix Up & Drink Up:

Ralph Stott Legends for Lunch Time

Richard A Rousay Choose the Right Walk With Noah:
Choose The Right and Walk With Ruth
Choose The Right Walk with Alma:

Robert Hewett Sr. - Down The Road We Came,
Thunderfoot:

Roger L. Scott - Letters from the Hills, The Last Trail Ride,
The Gifts of Pendrall:

Rochelle E. Fischer - Mystery In The Mist:
William Garret & Rochelle Fischer - Rosewood,
Poems & Promises:

*All these Authors can be seen on their own web-page along with their books at

www.apfpublisher.com

The Writers & Poetry Alliance

"The Cyber Home for All Who Love to Put Pen to Paper"
(To express thoughts, dreams and every inspiration)

apfpublisher@gmail.com

www.ingramcontent.com/pod-product-compliance
Ingram Content Group UK Ltd.
Pitfield, Milton Keynes, MK11 3LW, UK
UKHW041924190726
13854UKWH00003B/1437